Ingredients of a Balanced Diet

Seeds & Nuts

Rachel Eugster

FRANKLIN
WATTS

First published in 2007 by
Franklin Watts
338 Euston Road,
London NW1 3BH

Franklin Watts Australia
Hachette Children's Books
Level 17/207 Kent Street
Sydney NSW 2000

INGREDIENTS OF A BALANCED DIET:
SEEDS & NUTS was produced for Franklin
Watts by Bender Richardson White, PO Box
266, Uxbridge, UK.
Editor and Picture Researcher: Lionel Bender
Designer and Page Make-up: Ben White
Cover Make-up: Mike Pilley, Radius
Production: Kim Richardson
Graphics and Maps: Stefan Chabluk

A CIP catalogue record for this book is
available from the British Library.

ISBN: 978 0 7496 6899 0
Dewey classification: 641.3

Printed in China

Note to parents and teachers: Every effort has
been made by the Publishers to ensure that the
websites in this book are suitable for children,
that they are of the highest educational value,
and that they contain no inappropriate or
offensive material. However, because of the
nature of the Internet, it is impossible to
guarantee that the contents of these sites will
not be altered. We strongly advise that Internet
access is supervised by a responsible adult.

Franklin Watts is a division of Hachette
Children's Books

Picture credits

foodanddrinkphotos.com: pages 4, 13 top, 14, 22.
iStockphotos: pages 1, 3, 30, 31, 32 and all Food
bite panels; pages 1 bottom (David Coder); pages 3
and 27 top (Mario Fritzsche); page 14 and all
Recipe boxes (Molly Courtright); pages 5
(Slawomir Fajer); 7 left (Sergey Kashkin); 7 right
(Kelly Cline); 8 (Mara Cole Mat Greiner);
10(Vasko Mikovic); 11a and b (Kelly Cline); 12
(José Carlos Pires Pereira); 13 right (Elke
Dennis); 15 (Nathalie Dulex); 17 (boomzfoto); 18
(Adeline Lim); 19 (Cathleen Clapper); 20 (G. M.
Nicholas); 21 (Caroline K. Smith); 25; 27 bottom
(Martin de Wit).
Cover image: foodanddrinkphotos.com.
BRW wishes to thank Sarah Bell and colleagues at
foodanddrinkphotos.com for setting up the
commissioned photography.

The author
Rachel Eugster is a food, health and
nutrition writer and editor. Formerly
food editor of *Walking* magazine, she is
a regular contributor to *Continental*
and *YES Mag* and creates recipes for
people of all ages. She feeds her family
as healthy a diet as they will eat!

The consultant
Ester Davies is a professional food and
nutrition writer, lecturer and consultant.
She has a B.Ed. in Food, Nutrition and
Sociology. She has written books on food
specifically for the National Curriculum.

Note: In recipes, liquid measures and small
quantities are given by volume in millilitres
(ml) as this is how measuring jugs and
spoons are usually marked.

Contents

Nuts, seeds and fruits

Among the many types of plant foods we eat are seeds and nuts. While they make up no more than about 5 to 10% of our diet, seeds and nuts are important sources of nutrients and energy. Nutrients are chemicals our bodies need but cannot make themselves. Energy gives our bodies fuel. It powers our muscles and nerves and makes body processes work.

▼ Nuts and seeds range in size from the tiny seeds used to make spices such as pepper, to grains and the relatively enormous coconut.

coconut

peppercorns

Nutrition facts

Major nutrients

Sugars and starches, or carbohydrates: give you energy for action. Fibre, or roughage, is a kind of carbohydrate that aids digestion. Nuts and seeds are rich in carbohydrates.

Proteins: provide building materials for bones, hair, muscles and skin. There are many proteins in both nuts and seeds.

Vitamins and minerals: together these help you fight disease, digest food and strengthen your bones and teeth. Nuts and seeds contain a wide variety of these.

Fats: store energy for later use and carry vitamins to where they are needed. Nuts and seeds are sources of healthy plant (unsaturated) fats.

Are they nuts or seeds?

The word 'nut' is used both for any kind of fruit with a hard, woody shell and for the dry, edible nutmeat, kernel or seed inside the shell. A fruit is a seed-carrier produced by a flowering plant, and a seed is a part of a plant that can develop and grow into a new plant. Nuts that we eat include walnuts, almonds, cashews, pecans, sweet chestnuts, pistachios and macadamias.

Plants such as pine and fir trees also produce woody structures with seeds, but the seeds are not enclosed in a shell. The plant structures are called cones. Some people eat the seeds of pine cones. 'Pine nuts' is one name incorrectly given to these seeds because with no shell, they are not nuts.

Peanuts are eaten as nuts but are really seeds. They are related to beans, peas and lentils, which are also seeds (see the panel to the right). Other seeds we eat include sunflower, sesame, poppy and caraway seeds. We also eat grains, such as wheat, barley, oats, maize and rice, which are the seeds of cereal plants. Dried beans, peas and lentils – together called pulses – and grains are dealt with in separate books in this series.

Food bites

Edible connections

Nuts are edible fruits. So, too, are legumes, or pods, which contain seeds we call beans, peas or lentils. Apples and pears are soft, fleshy fruits. Oranges, lemons and grapefruits are soft, watery fruits known as citrus fruits. Peppers and cucumbers are fruits eaten as vegetables.

In diet terms and cooking, the word 'seeds' is usually used for edible seeds that are neither grains or nuts. They include sunflower, flax and sesame seeds. The oils from these seeds are often used for cooking and to make margarine.

◀ Peanuts develop inside a legume or pod. At first the pod is soft and fleshy, but as it is pushed below ground by the plant, it becomes dry and hard like a nut shell.

Nutrition facts

The main food groups:

1. Bread and other grain products, and potatoes. These are rich in carbohydrates (including fibre), proteins, minerals and vitamins.

2. Fruits and vegetables. All of these are rich in carbohydrates (including fibre), vitamins and minerals.

3. Meat, fish, shellfish, eggs, seeds, nuts and pulses. These are good sources of proteins, minerals and B vitamins. Red meat includes lamb, beef, veal and pork. White meat comes from poultry, which includes chickens and turkeys.

4. Milk and dairy products. These are good sources of calcium and proteins but are often high in unhealthy saturated (animal) fats.

5. Fatty, sugary and salty foods. These contain unhealthy saturated fats, salt and lots of energy.

Food groups

Your diet is everything you eat and drink, from main meals and snacks to an ice cream and a glass of tap water. Balancing your diet means eating the right amounts of healthy foods, avoiding unhealthy foods, and taking in only as much energy as your body needs.

To help you choose what to eat and drink, food scientists have created diagrams that group ingredients according to their nutrients. Examples of these are the food pyramid and food plate shown below.

Food pyramid and food plate

On this food pyramid, nuts and seeds are placed halfway up. This means you should eat neither too much nor too little of them. You should eat mostly foods from the bottom of the pyramid and only a little of those from the top. Most of your meals should resemble the food plate. Fill one-quarter with protein-rich foods, such as meat, nuts or seeds, and fill the rest with other foods.

◀ Several spices that we use to add flavours to our foods come from seeds. They include fennel, coriander, pepper, mustard, poppy and cumin.

▲ A breakfast treat of a mixture of grains, coconut, raisins, fresh fruit and yogurt. You may also add seeds and nuts to your favourite breakfast cereal.

Making meals

Choosing the right ingredients from a food pyramid or food plate is one step to building a balanced diet. Next, the ingredients must be used to make dishes that are nutritious and tasty. Seeds and nuts can be an important part of this.

Most people eat seeds and nuts as snacks or toppings for salads, in stews or as flavourings in cooking. Seeds other than grains are a major source of vegetable oils used for cooking and to make salad dressings, biscuits and cakes. This book will illustrate these and other uses as part of a balanced diet.

More about nutrients

Proteins are made of chemicals known as amino acids. Some amino acids can be made in your body, others cannot, or at least not in sufficient amounts to keep you healthy. You must get these amino acids from your diet. Seeds and nuts are rich in proteins but they lack some of these essential amino acids. The missing amino acids are present in fish, dairy products, eggs, some grains and some pulses.

Nuts, especially, are rich in fats. There are two types of fats: saturated and unsaturated. In your diet, you must include some unsaturated fats but you should avoid saturated fats as they can lead to heart disorders. Seeds and nuts contain unsaturated fats. However, too much fat of any kind may not be used up quickly. When extra fat is stored in your body, you put on weight.

Nutrition facts

Vitamin needs

Vitamin A is for healthy eyes, blood and bones
B vitamins prevent heart disease and some cancers
Vitamin C prevents and fights infections
Vitamin D is for healthy bones and prevents cancer
Vitamin E prevents cell damage
Vitamin K is for healthy blood and bones

Seeds and nuts are good sources of B vitamins and also they contain vitamins A, E and K. They contain no vitamins C or D.

◀Grilled salmon and green salad topped with nuts. This dish is rich in proteins, minerals and vitamins.

Nutrient levels

A comparison of the nutrient content of some nuts, seeds and other foods. The lengths of the sections show the proportions of each nutrient. Water is a nutrient, too, as your body cannot make as much as it needs.

chicken, roast

almonds

coconut

peanuts, roasted

beef sausage

| protein | fats | carbohydrates | water |

Oils, minerals and other chemicals

Seeds and nuts are good sources of essential fatty acids – healthy unsaturated fats the body needs but cannot make itself. These exist as oils, which are fats that are liquid at normal temperatures.

Seeds and nuts also provide many minerals and vitamins (see panels to the left and right). Some minerals allow enzymes to work. Enzymes are proteins that control your body's chemical processes, for example digestion (see pages 22-23). Seeds and nuts also contain phytochemicals, which work together to keep you healthy, and some fibre.

Food bites

Mineral-rich almonds

Raw or roasted, chopped or ground, almonds can be used in snacks, salads and main dishes. They have as much protein, eight times the calcium, twice the iron and twice the potassium as a cooked beefburger of the same weight.

The mineral calcium is needed for healthy teeth and bones. Without it, these become brittle and can break easily.

Iron is needed for healthy red blood cells. These cells carry oxygen round the body. Oxygen is essential for the body's chemical processes to work.

Potassium controls water balance in the body and is needed for healthy muscles and nerve cells.

Nutrition facts

A favourite seed worldwide

We call them coffee beans but they are not beans because they do not come from a plant pod. Coffee beans are the seeds of a berry type of fruit. Coffee (the drink) is made by pouring hot water over ground coffee beans. Over 400 billion cups of coffee are drunk worldwide every year.

Coffee may have health benefits, but it contains caffeine, a chemical that can make you over-active and prevent you sleeping well. Caffeine is also added to some soft drinks. You should not drink large amounts of caffeinated drinks. Caffeine can be removed from coffee, but you should still drink it only in small amounts.

Already in your diet

Seeds and nuts are often used as additions to other dishes, rather than being the featured ingredients. For example, baked goods – cakes, biscuits and scones – often contain nuts. Seeds are used for baked goods, too – think of the seeds sprinkled on hamburger buns, bagels and bread.

◀ Some bagels are coated with sesame, poppy or celery seeds or a mix of all three.

In salads and spreads

Vegetable and fruit dishes are sometimes made more interesting by the addition of nuts or seeds, as in mixed bean salads and Waldorf salad – a mixture of apples, celery, walnuts and raisins. Also, every time you spread peanut butter or a chocolate-hazelnut spread on your bread, you are eating nuts.

A variety of prepared and ready-made meals contain nuts. These include certain chocolate and cereal bars, ice creams, cakes, pastries and Far Eastern and Indian dishes. Seeds are often added to breads and biscuits.

Upgrading what you eat

To add more seeds and nuts to your diet, try sprinkling chopped pecans on your porridge or cold cereals. Add toasted sunflower seeds to salads for some crunch and a nice nutty flavour. Dry-roasted sunflower seeds or nuts such as pistachios or cashews are a satisfying snack that is much better for you than potato crisps. When you bake scones, toss some chopped walnuts or almonds into the dough to boost nutrition and flavour.

Snacks

A handful of seeds and nuts makes a great snack on its own, or mixed with dried fruit. Try cashew nuts, walnuts, pistachios, pecans, peanuts or sunflower seeds. To avoid added salt and saturated fat, choose nuts or seeds that are unsalted, and which are either raw or dry-roasted.

▼ A pecan pie. Eat only small portions of nut pies as they are rich in energy-high sugars and fats and are very filling.

▲ Nuts go well with cheeses as a snack or dessert.

Prepared in many ways

There are many other ways you can eat seeds and nuts beyond peanut butter and bun toppings. Roasted nuts and seeds make flavoursome toppings for cereals, vegetables, fish and salads. For information on roasting nuts see page 27.

Some people use nut stuffings for roast chicken and roast turkey. The stuffings help to keep the meat moist during cooking, and the nutty flavours make the meal more tasty. Puréed chestnuts and shelled and chopped walnuts, cashews and Brazils are good choices for these.

▲ Roasted chestnuts can be eaten as a snack. Once cooked, the shell and thin skin around each nut should be removed. These are sweet chestnuts. Horse chestnuts (conkers) are not edible.

Nutrition facts

Sunflower seeds

As their name suggests, sunflower seeds are the seeds of the big, bright yellow sunflower. Originally from Mexico and Peru, sunflower plants are now found all over the world. Russia and Ukraine grow the largest amounts.

Sunflower seeds are full of essential fatty acids, fibre, protein, vitamin E and minerals such as magnesium and selenium. Sunflowers are most often eaten as snacks or pressed to release their oil, which is one of the most popular oils in the world.

The protein-rich cake of squashed sunflower seeds left behind after the oil is removed is a valuable food source for farm animals.

▼ Brittle bars and cookies are made with a variety of seeds and nuts. These snack foods are very nutritious but high in energy, so do not make them a frequent part of your diet.

Flour and brittle

Nuts can also be ground and used instead of flour – in a cake, for example. Nuts are used in many kinds of sweets, too. Peanut and cashew brittle are little more than caramelised sugar and nuts. Halvah is a Middle Eastern sweet made from ground sesame seeds, or sometimes almonds. Chestnuts are also used for many sweets, ground, sugar-coated or puréed.

Butters

Peanut butter may be the most popular nut spread but many other nuts and seeds are ground into butters. These include cashews, almonds, hazelnuts, Brazil nuts, pistachios, macadamias, walnuts, pumpkin seeds, sunflower seeds and even hemp seeds. When sesame seeds are ground into butter the result is called tahini, an important ingredient in Middle Eastern cooking.

Trying different varieties of nuts and seeds and new ways of eating them will give you a varied mixture of nutrients, which is needed for a balanced diet.

Multi-purpose peanut

George Washington Carver was a US inventor who was born a slave in around 1861. He discovered more than 300 uses for the peanut, including a type of milk, face powder, printer's ink and soap. From Carver's time, ground peanuts have been used to make nut butter, bread and to flavour ice creams.

▲ Peanut butter is eaten as a spread, as an addition to soups and salads, and in desserts.

Roasty toasty muesli

Makes 6 to 8 servings.
Ingredients
200g rolled oats
75g each of raw slivered almonds,
   sunflower seeds, cashews,
   pecans, pumpkin seeds (shelled)
60g flax seeds
120ml sunflower, rapeseed or flax
   oil
120ml honey
75g each of dried cherries, dried
   cranberries, raisins

Preparation
Preheat the oven to 170°C (Gas
   mark 3).
Mix the first seven ingredients.
   Warm the honey a little in a
   saucepan, and stir in the oil.
   Drizzle this mixture over the
   oats, nuts and seeds. Mix well.
Spread the mixture on a baking
   tray. Bake, stirring every 5 or
   10 minutes, until the muesli is
   golden. Be careful not to let it
   burn.
Remove the muesli from the oven,
   stir in the dried fruit, and allow
   it to cool. When cool, stir it
   once again to break up the
   clumps, and store it in an
   airtight container.
Serve with low-fat milk or yogurt
   for breakfast or a snack.

Oils and sprouts

Seeds and nuts are rich in vegetable oils, which is a general name for liquid fats that we get from plants. Edible vegetable oils come from nuts such as walnuts and peanuts, and from seeds such as rapeseed, sunflower, flax and cotton. A popular vegetable oil, canola, is made from a type of rapeseed. Canola has less saturated fat than other vegetable oils.

Vegetable oils are used for cooking and in such food products as margarines, salad dressings and mayonnaises — mixes of oils, egg yolks, mustard and spices. Vegetables oils are healthiest in liquid form.

▼ Vegetable oils made from seeds and nuts. They differ in taste, thickness and colour.

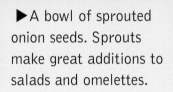

►A bowl of sprouted onion seeds. Sprouts make great additions to salads and omelettes.

Nutrition facts

Sprout juice

Alfalfa sprouts can be made into a juice. For best results, use a special vegetable juicer. The sprouts are a good source of protein and the minerals calcium, magnesium, potassium, silicon, cobalt and zinc. Most of these minerals are needed for enzymes to work properly (see page 9).

Extracting the oils

There are two main ways of extracting vegetable oils from seeds and nuts. The first involves soaking them in a liquid that draws the oils from the plant material and then warming the mixture to remove the liquid. The second method involves pressing down hard on the seeds and nuts to squeeze out the oils.

During these processes, some of the nutrients naturally present in the oils are removed, and the original flavour and colour of the oils are changed. However, plenty of nutrients remain in the oils.

Eating sprouts

Some seeds can be eaten as sprouts, which are young, germinating plants. They include mung beans, sunflower, alfalfa, peanuts, barley and flax seeds. The sprouts have different mixes of nutrients to the seeds themselves and make great additions to sandwiches, stir-fries and salads. You can find details of how to grow your own sprouts from seeds on some of the websites listed on page 31.

African peanut stew

Makes 4 servings.
Ingredients
450g sirloin beef, in chunks
45ml rapeseed or olive oil
1 onion, chopped
1 sweet green pepper, chopped
2 large tomatoes, diced
60ml peanut butter, crunchy-type*
120ml water
2.5ml cayenne pepper

Preparation
Heat 30ml of the oil in a saucepan then brown the meat in the oil. Add enough water to cover the meat and simmer until it is tender. Remove the saucepan from the heat.

In a separate pan, sauté the pepper and onions in the remaining 15ml of oil. Add the diced tomatoes. Blend the peanut butter with the 120ml water and add to the vegetables. Add the cayenne and meat (with its juices). Let the mixture simmer for 15 minutes over a low heat.

Serve with rice, sweet potatoes, and spinach, chard or collards.

*Be sure to use peanut butter that contains nothing but ground-up peanuts.

Around the world

Most edible seeds and nuts come from warm or hot regions of the world. The main nut-growing countries are China, India, Australia, the United States, Mexico, South Africa, France, Italy, Spain and Turkey. Brazil nuts come from the Amazon river region of South America. Edible seeds, including grains and pulses, are grown as major crops in these countries and in Canada, Russia, Japan and Britain.

Spices around the world

This map shows the native, or original, countries of many seeds that are used as spices.

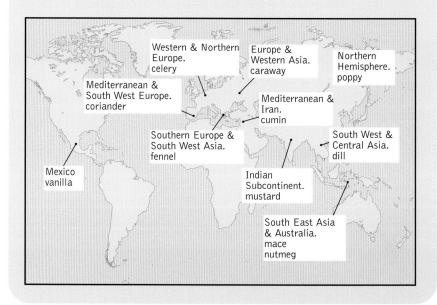

Western & Northern Europe. celery

Europe & Western Asia. caraway

Northern Hemisphere. poppy

Mediterranean & South West Europe. coriander

Mediterranean & Iran. cumin

Southern Europe & South West Asia. fennel

South West & Central Asia. dill

Mexico vanilla

Indian Subcontinent. mustard

South East Asia & Australia. mace nutmeg

Nutrition facts

Lesser-known seeds and nuts and their uses:

Alfalfa seeds Sprouted for salads, sandwiches and to make a juice

Beechnut Used for chewing gum flavouring

Breadnut tree seeds (or maya nuts) Eaten stewed, fresh, dried or roasted

Candlenut Grown for oil; eaten in Malaysian and Indonesian cooking

Chestnut Roasted, sugar-coated or ground into flour

Cottonseed Used in salad and for an oil for cooking and to make cake mixtures and margarines

Flax seed or linseed Used as oil, or added to breads and soups

Lotus seeds Eaten raw, dried or popped

Melon and squash seeds Roasted and eaten as a snack

Safflower seeds Used mainly for oil

Peanuts for all

In Europe and North America, the peanut appears primarily as a snack or as peanut butter. In parts of Central and West Africa, the peanut is a staple food.

In Asian cuisines, the peanut is used frequently. Pad Thai is a noodle dish garnished with chopped peanuts. A peanut sauce is often used on satay, which is barbecued spiced meat cooked on skewers. Both these dishes are popular in Thailand. In South America, where the peanut originated, it is eaten raw or roasted, and is made into peanut soup, peanut milk and sweets.

Macadamia nuts

The macadamia nut comes from Australia, but is now widely grown and used in Hawaii, Kenya, Brazil, Israel and parts of the United States. It tastes sweet and is highly nutritious. Macadamia nuts can be eaten raw or roasted or coated in chocolate. They can be used in cakes, ground into butter, or for their oil.

▼ The story of the macadamia nut, from the fleshy, green fruit to dry nut and loose kernel.

Suggestions for meals

Salt and spices

Too much salt in your diet can lead to high blood pressure. You can reduce the amount of salt you eat without ever missing it if you make changes gradually.

Exploring the use of spices will help you. The seeds we use as spices offer an impressive array of flavours. Some spices – which can be from the root, bark or seeds of plants – are used for sweets. These include cinnamon, nutmeg and cloves. Cumin, pepper and mustard are used for spicy dishes. Ginger can be used for either, as can chocolate.

You may be amazed at how much better food tastes when it has less salt and more flavour.

Any healthy food you eat replaces unhealthy food and provides better nutrients. Here are some more tasty ways to eat seeds and nuts.

Breakfast, snacks and lunch

For breakfast, add chopped macadamias, pecans or almonds to bread, pancakes or waffles. Mix chopped walnuts and cinnamon with cream cheese and spread this on bagels, toast or crackers.

Seeds and nuts work well in snack foods, too. Try mixing seeds and nuts with dried fruit. For interest and variety, add mini-marshmallows or chocolate chips – but in small amounts. Slivered almonds or chopped pistachios make a great topping for blue cheese, brie and other cheeses. Pair this with bread or crackers for a snack or for lunch. Make a cheese ball by mixing grated cheese with nuts and a little cream cheese.

▼ Chocolate brownies topped with scattered crushed nuts make a filling snack or dessert and are tasty for an occasional treat.

Dinner ideas

For a salad – as a main course or a side dish – vary the popular almond-and-green bean combination. Try chopped hazelnuts or Brazil nuts on broccoli, carrots or cauliflower. Pine nuts and raisins are a particularly delicious addition to spinach.

For a traditional Italian sauce to go with pasta, purée pine nuts with garlic, basil and olive oil, and add some grated Parmesan cheese. Most nuts go well with almost any kind of pasta dish, and will add nutrients and flavour. Nuts can also be used to garnish soup, salads, casseroles and grain dishes.

Dress up breadcrumb toppings and stuffings by adding chopped nuts and spices. Or roll meat, fish or poultry in this mixture before baking or grilling.

When it comes to desserts, seeds and nuts can be added to baked goods, sprinkled on ice creams or sorbets, or added to fruit salad.

Recipe

Brazil nut apricot scones

Makes 18 scones.

Ingredients
225g flour
50g rolled oats
10ml baking powder
25g sugar
180ml low-fat milk
60ml rapeseed oil
2 eggs
125g chopped Brazil nuts
100g chopped dried apricots

Preparation
Preheat the oven to 170°C (Gas mark 3) and grease a baking tray with oil.

Mix the flour, oats, baking powder and sugar in a bowl. Add the milk, oil and eggs, and stir to combine. Stir in the nuts and apricots.

Drop heaped spoonfuls of dough on to the tray. Bake for 15 minutes or until golden brown.

Serve with jam, cream cheese or chocolate hazelnut spread.

◀ Toasted almonds go well with runner beans.

Pecan rice roast

Makes 4 servings

Ingredients
15ml olive oil
1 onion, chopped
1 stalk celery, chopped
175g cooked rice
125g pecans
1 egg, beaten
3 sprigs parsley, chopped
15ml Worcestershire sauce
pepper, to taste

Preparation
Preheat the oven to 190°C (Gas mark 5). Warm the olive oil in a frying pan, and sauté the onion and celery until soft (3 to 5 minutes). Stir in all remaining ingredients. Turn into a greased casserole dish. Bake for 30 minutes.
Serve with hot sauce or chutney if desired.

▶ A savoury pancake filled with a mixture of nuts and vegetables and topped with peanuts. Eaten with salad, this makes a tasty nutritious vegetarian dish.

Vegetarian meals

V egetarians are people who do not eat meat. Many vegetarians avoid eating meat because they believe it is wrong to kill animals for food. Others believe a vegetarian diet is healthier, or their religion forbids them from eating meat. In poor parts of the world, some people are vegetarians only because they cannot afford meat or it is not available in shops and markets. Meat is a good source of proteins so vegetarians must get proteins from plant foods such as seeds and nuts instead.

Some vegetarians will drink milk and eat dairy products and eggs while others will not eat eggs but include milk and dairy products in their diet. People who will not eat or drink any animal products at all are known as vegans.

Getting all the nutrients

If you are a vegetarian, you must plan carefully to be sure to get all the amino acids, vitamins and minerals you need. Eat a wide variety of seeds and nuts, as well as whole grains, pulses, vegetables and fruit. This will supply all the nutrients you need to balance your diet. Low-fat dairy foods are also important.

Vegetarian meals

Many of the nut and seed dishes already discussed in this book do not include meat. As a vegetarian, you can eat these. You can make a soup by heating water, yogurt and flour in a saucepan and adding ground fenugreek seeds and chopped walnuts. For a curry dish, mix slices of pineapple with mustard seeds, coconut milk, herbs and spices. You can add almost any kind of chopped nuts and seeds to grain dishes and to green, leafy salads.

Walnuts, pecans, almonds and hazelnuts – whole, chopped or as pastes – can be used to make a variety of pies and pastries.

▲ A healthy salad, dressed up with seeds and nuts.

Nutrition facts

Vegan options

Nut and seed (including grain) sources for nutrients most people get from animal foods:

Vitamins:	Minerals:
vitamin A cashews, pecans	**calcium** nuts, sesame and sunflower seeds
vitamin B1 hazelnuts, oats, wholemeal bread	**copper** most nuts and whole grains
vitamin B3 peanuts, sesame seeds	**iron** cashews, almonds, whole grains
vitamin B5 peanuts, bran	**magnesium** most nuts and grains
vitamin B9 some seeds, wholemeal bread	**phosphorus** most nuts and grains
vitamin E most nuts, vegetable oils, cereals	**zinc** almonds, Brazils, pecans, whole grains

Nutrition facts

Food allergies

Sometimes, a person's body reacts as if a particular food were attacking it, like a poison. Eating a food you are allergic to may make you itchy or nauseous or make breathing difficult.

About 1 in 130 people are allergic to nuts. Many schools ask parents to avoid sending lunches or snacks containing nuts to school with their children. But nuts are sometimes included in foods where you would not expect them to be.

Even foods that do not contain nuts can be a problem if they are produced in the same kitchen or factory where nuts are processed. If you have an allergy, always check food labels carefully.

Using what you eat

Nutrition is the study of foods and drinks and how your body uses them. Digestion is the process your body uses to break down the foods and drinks in your diet to release the nutrients and energy within them. Seeds and nuts tend to be digested more slowly than many other foods as they are particularly rich in nutrients – especially proteins and some healthy unsaturated fats.

▼ Because you digest them slowly, nut bars are a good way to keep up your energy levels.

Slow breakdown

Digestion starts as you cut, tear and grind food into a mash or pulp using your teeth and tongue. In the next step, chemicals known as enzymes slowly break down proteins, fats and carbohydrates into small units. The enzymes are added to the mash in your mouth, stomach and small intestines. Digestion ends as the nutrients enter your bloodstream. Fibre is left undigested and later removes waste from your system.

Food bites

Health facts

The digestive system

Your digestive tube, running from your mouth to your anus, has muscular walls. As the walls contract, food is pushed through the system. Enzymes are added along the way. Digestion can take 24 hours to complete.

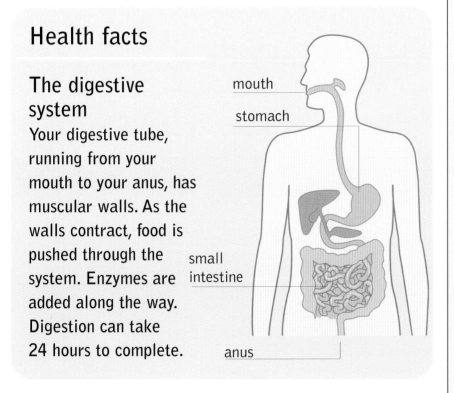

mouth

stomach

small intestine

anus

Food as fuel

The broken-down food material is carried round your body. Some of it is used for growth and the repair of cells. The rest is used as a fuel to provide energy for your muscles to work. In the process, heat and water are produced. The heat keeps your body warm. The water is needed for cells to work properly. The rest of the water you get rid of when you go to the toilet.

Eating imbalances

Your body will usually help you to keep a balanced diet. If you eat too much, your stomach will feel full and your appetite – your wish to eat – will be satisfied. If you do not eat enough, you will feel hungry. Your stomach may make rumbling noises and you may feel tired. If you do not drink enough, you may feel faint and get a headache.

If you eat too much and do not exercise enough, you may become obese, or very overweight. Some people think they are too fat but eat far too little. They are known as anorexic. Others eat too much, then make themselves sick so as not to digest the food. Their weight is usually low. These people are said to be bulimic.

Food bites

Daily energy needs

infants aged 3-4
    about 1,600 kcal
children aged 7-10
    about 2,000 kcal
girls aged 11-14
    about 2,200 kcal
boys aged 11-14
    about 2,500 kcal
women, between 2,200 and
    2,600 kcal
men, between 2,600 and
    3,600 kcal
    1 kcal = 4.2 kJ.

Looking and feeling good

I f you eat a healthy, balanced diet and exercise regularly, you will look and feel good. You will take only as much energy from foods and drinks as you need. The energy figures on the left are for average, healthy children. If you are growing fast or are fighting an illness, you may need more energy than usual. You will find more details on recommended energy needs on some of the websites listed on page 31.

Counting calories

The energy content of foods and drinks is usually measured in kilocalories (kcal) or kilojoules (kJ) – 'kilo' meaning 1,000. Compared with other foods, nuts

Body

Choose the correct chart. For your age, see where you are on the graph. If your weight is close to the red line marking the average weight, that is fine. If not, you need to balance your diet more carefully or seek advice.

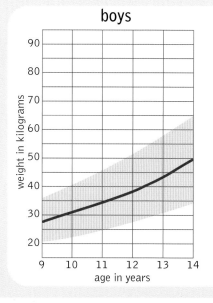

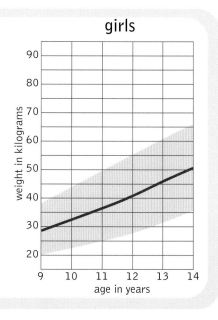

24

and seeds are energy-rich: 100g of roasted almonds contains 597kcal compared to 331 for the same weight of fried potato chips, 141 for tinned salmon, 299 for beef sausages and 497 for chocolate biscuits. Almonds, though, are more nutritious than foods such as chips or biscuits.

Energy balance

The chart to the right shows the energy content for a one-day menu. You will see that is perfectly possible to eat a peanut butter sandwich and have a nut biscuit for dessert without taking in too many kilocalories.

However, unless recommended by a doctor or dietician, you should not need to weigh everything you eat and drink and work out the energy content.

Food bites

A day's worth of energy

kcal	meals
	breakfast
190	1 bowl oatmeal cereal with 2 teaspoons honey
105	1 banana
105	1 glass orange juice
	lunch
360	peanut butter and strawberry jam sandwich on multigrain bread
96	1 pear
102	1 glass semi-skimmed milk
	snack
249	$1/3$ cup roasted sunflower seeds
	dinner
177	1 glass apple juice
233	100g grilled salmon
166	1 cup wild rice
129	1 cup green beans sprinkled with sliced, toasted almonds
134	1 oatmeal-pecan biscuit
2,046	**GRAND TOTAL**

▼ Everything you do uses up energy — working, playing, doing sport or just resting and sleeping.

Nutrition facts

Shelf life

Seeds and nuts should be stored in airtight containers or sealed plastic bags in a cool, dry, dark place. Because they are high in oils, which can go off after some months, some seeds and nuts are best kept in the refrigerator or freezer. Those that have gone mouldy or smell off should be thrown away.

Shopping and cooking

You can buy seeds and nuts in most food shops and supermarkets, and at food market stalls. They come loose or packed in bags, whole or shelled. Some are more readily available at certain times of the year. You can also get most seeds and nuts of all kinds from Internet food stores.

Read the labels

Nuts keep best in their shells. When you buy them, look for clean, unopened shells without cracks. This does not apply to pistachios, which are usually sold in

▶ Most food and drink packages have labels telling you the nutrients and energy in the products. Use this information to choose foods that are high in fibre, minerals and vitamins and to avoid products that you are allergic to (see page 22).

Ingredients

Brazil Nuts (35%), Almonds (25%), Hazelnuts (25%), Walnut Halves (15%).
Packaged in a protective atmosphere.

Nutrition

Typical Composition	100g (3.5 oz) provide
Energy	**2575kj**
	625kcal
Protein	**18.8g**
Carbohydrate	**4.5g**
of which sugars	3.4g
Fat	**58.5g**
of which saturates	5.5g
Fibre	**5.5g**
Sodium	**0.0g**
Vitamins/Minerals	
Vitamin E	**14.9mg (149%RDA**

RDA = Recommended Daily Alowance

A display of loose nuts, including Brazils, hazelnuts, walnuts and almonds.

partially opened shells. If you are buying seeds and nuts in packets, check the 'sell by' or 'best before' dates on the wrapping or label.

Nut-free food products are sometimes processed on equipment that is also used for foods that do contain nuts. A message like 'may contain traces of nuts' may appear on packages as an alert.

Roasting or toasting

Raw nuts and seeds can be made more tasty by roasting or toasting them. To roast small nuts and seeds, sprinkle them evenly over a baking tray and put them in an oven at 180°C (Gas mark 4) for about 8 minutes. They can also be toasted in a dry frying pan over a medium heat while being stirred constantly to keep them from burning. Nuts such as walnuts, almonds and pecans should be shelled first. With chestnuts, pierce the shells first to stop them exploding in the oven and roast them for 30 minutes. You can also roast chestnuts on an open fire or barbecue.

Cracking nuts

The shells of nuts such as Brazils are very hard to break. The shells can be softened by freezing the nuts or by steaming or boiling them in water for about three minutes. If you use heat, put nuts in cold water before trying to break them open with a nutcracker.

Use a nutcracker to open tough nuts such as walnuts.

Cooking safety

Here are some rules you should follow when cooking and following recipes.

- ask an adult for permission to cook and for help in handling anything sharp or hot
- wash your hands before you begin
- after handling raw meat, wash your hands, cooking tools and surfaces with hot, soapy water
- wash fruits and vegetables before using
- use pot holders or oven gloves when handling something hot
- keep pot handles turned towards the back of the stove
- open pan lids away from you to avoid burning your face with steam
- avoid loose long sleeves, or roll them up
- keep your fingers and hair out of the way when using appliances
- never plug in appliances with wet hands

Projects

Here are some ideas for things you can do related to eating seeds and nuts. Discover the variety of seeds and nuts that are available to you. Record what you are eating now and see how you can eat more seeds and nuts to better balance your diet.

Action 1

Supermarket detective

- How many different kinds of seeds and nuts in packets can you find in your local supermarket?
- For each kind, make a list of the various forms it comes in: shelled, unshelled, whole, sliced, chopped, ground, plain and roasted. Which is the most common kind and form of nut and seed?
- Look at the packaging labels to find out which countries the seeds and nuts came from. Do some countries seem to produce more seeds and nuts than others and, if so, is this what you expected?
- Go to the ready-made meals section of the supermarket. By reading the labels on the products, record how many of them contain seeds and nuts.
- How many labels on packaging contain warnings about nut allergies? Are the warnings clear?
- Are some food labels better than others? Work out why and discuss this with your friends and parents.

Action 2

Food tracking

Make a chart like the one shown below. For five days, every time you eat seeds and nuts or a product that contains them, put a tick into the appropriate box or boxes. At the end of the five days, count the number of ticks for each ingredient. Write these totals in the right-hand column. Now, add up how many times you ate nuts and seeds each day.

Ingredient:	Monday	Tuesday	Wednesday	Thursday	Friday	Weekly total
seeds on their own						
nuts on their own						
seeds mixed in						
nuts mixed in						
cereals with nuts/seeds						
seed or nut bars						
TOTAL seeds & nuts						

- How many times during the five days did you eat nuts and seeds?
- Was this more or less than you expected?
- On how many occasions did you eat nuts and/or seeds as a snack?
- Did you eat most of your nuts and seeds in breakfast cereals?
- Do you think you ate the right amount for a balanced diet? If not, how can you change your diet?

Action 3

New seeds and nuts

What seeds and nuts do you eat now? How many others are listed in this book? Next time you go shopping, see if you can find some new seeds and nuts to try.

Are some seeds and nuts available in the shops only at certain times of the year? Can you think of any reasons why? Do more of the seeds and nuts come from Asia, Africa and South America than from the rest of the world? Why do you think this is?

Discuss with your friends the different seeds and nuts you eat. Do they eat the same nuts and seeds as you? What are your favourite seeds and nuts and what are theirs? Discuss your reasons why.

Glossary

CARBOHYDRATES
One of the three main nutrients in food. They are made of sugar molecules and mostly provide energy.

CHEMICALS
Substances made of atoms and molecules. Nutrients and enzymes are chemicals.

ENZYMES
Substances that make chemical processes work.

FATS
One of the three main nutrients in food. They are made of fatty acids and glycerol and mostly provide an energy store.

GRAINS
The seeds of grass plants.

INGREDIENTS
Items of food used to cook a dish.

KILOCALORIES
The units used to measure the energy in foods and drinks.

MINERALS
Nutrients needed for health. They include iron, calcium, sodium and zinc.

NUTRIENTS
Materials the body needs but cannot make itself.

OILS
Fats that are normally liquid at room temperatures.

PHYTOCHEMICALS
Substances present in plant foods that protect the body against diseases.

POULTRY
Birds kept for meat and eggs, in particular chickens, turkeys and ducks. Their meat is called 'white meat' to contrast with red meat.

PROTEINS
One of the three main nutrients in food. They are made of amino acids and mostly provide building materials for the body.

PULSES
Dried beans, peas and lentils.

RED MEAT
Meat rich in blood, in particular beef, lamb, veal, pork and venison.

SATURATED FATS
Fats found mainly in animal foods. Eating too much saturated fat can raise the levels of cholesterol in your blood, increasing the risk of heart disease.

SEEDS
Parts of plants that can develop and grow into new plants. Seeds form within fruits.

STAPLE
Any food that forms a large part of people's diet.

VITAMINS
Nutrients needed in small quantities for health, fitness and body processes.

Websites

Here is a selection of websites that have information and activities about food, diet, health and fitness.
Some deal only with seeds and nuts. Others are more general but include seeds and nuts.

http://www.bbc.co.uk/food/back_to_
  basics/nuts.shtml
Fun facts about specific seeds and nuts.

http://www.urbanext.uiuc.edu/gpe/
  case3/c3facts2.html
Help Detective Leplant investigate the mysteries of the seed.

http://www.nutripeople.co.uk/health
  notes_content.asp?ContentID=
  1848004
Recipes and information about specific seeds and nuts from a nutritionists' network.

http://www.nuthealth.org/
Nut information and recipes from the International Tree Nut Council Nutrition Research and Education Foundation.

http://www.vegsoc.org/info/nutsseeds.
  html
Nut and seed nutrition and storage information from the Vegetarian Society.

http://www.sproutpeople.com/grow/
  sprouting.html
All about sprouting seeds.

http://www.passionateaboutfood.net/
  healthy.php
A wide variety of information about food, with recipes and advice.

http://www.askdrsears.com/html/4/
  T043600.asp
Why and how to eat seeds and nuts, and how specific varieties compare.

http://www.thenutfactory.com/kitchen/
  edible.html
Information on unusual seeds and nuts from around the world.

http://www.foodafactoflife.org.uk/
Educational material about food, diet and nutrients.

Index